LYRICS FOR THE CENTURIES

Sermons For The Sundays
After Pentecost (First Third)
Cycle B, First Lesson Texts

Arthur H. Kolsti

CSS Publishing Company, Inc., Lima, Ohio

LYRICS FOR THE CENTURIES

Copyright © 1996 by
CSS Publishing Company, Inc.
Lima, Ohio

All rights reserved. No part of this publication may be reproduced in any manner whatsoever without the prior permission of the publisher, except in the case of brief quotations embodied in critical articles and reviews. Inquiries should be addressed to: Permissions, CSS Publishing Company, Inc., P.O. Box 4503, Lima, Ohio 45802-4503.

Scripture quotations are from the *New Revised Standard Version of the Bible,* copyright 1989 by the Division of Christian Education of the National Council of the Churches of Christ in the USA. Used by permission.

Library of Congress Cataloging-in-Publication Data

Kolsti, Arthur H., 1925-
    Lyrics for the centuries : sermons for the Sundays after Pentecost (first third) : cycle B, first lesson texts / Arthur H. Kolsti.
      p.   cm.
    ISBN 0-7880-0777-7 (pbk.)
    1. Pentecost season — Sermons. 2. Bible O.T. — Sermons. 3. Sermons, American. I. Title.
BV61.K649   1996
252'.6—dc20   96-10702
                                                                                      CIP

*To Josée
in this our
fiftieth anniversary year*

Table Of Contents

Pentecost   7
   Wind — Word — Spirit — Community
   Acts 2:1-21
   Ezekiel 37:1-14

Holy Trinity   13
   R.S.V.P.
   Isaiah 6:1-8

Proper 4   19
Pentecost 2
Corpus Christi
   Here Is Where It Happens
   1 Samuel 3:1-10 (11-20)

Proper 5   25
Pentecost 3
Ordinary Time 10
   Saul, The Tormented King
   1 Samuel 8:4-20 (11:14-15)

Proper 6   31
Pentecost 4
Ordinary Time 11
   When Saints Go Marching Forth
   1 Samuel 15:34—16:13

Proper 7   35
Pentecost 5
Ordinary Time 12
   Acquaintances Or Friends?
   1 Samuel 17:57—18:5, 10-16

Proper 8   41
Pentecost 6
Ordinary Time 13
    Lyrics For The Centuries
    2 Samuel 1:1, 17-27

Proper 9   47
Pentecost 7
Ordinary Time 14
    Another Kind Of Success
    2 Samuel 5:1-5, 9-10

Proper 10   51
Pentecost 8
Ordinary Time 15
    The Strange Tactics Of God
    2 Samuel 6:1-5, 12b-19

Proper 11   57
Pentecost 9
Ordinary Time 16
    A Habitat For Humanity
    2 Samuel 7:1-14a

Lectionary Preaching After Pentecost   61

Acts 2:1-21 Pentecost
Ezekiel 37:1-14

Wind — Word — Spirit — Community

Then he said to me, "Prophesy to these bones, and say to them: O dry bones, hear the word of the Lord to the breath, prophesy mortal, and say to the breath: Thus says the Lord God: Come from the four winds, O breath, and breathe upon these slain, that they may live." I prophesied as he commanded me, and the breath came into them, and they lived, and stood on their feet, a vast multitude.

— Ezekiel 37:4-10

And suddenly from heaven there came a sound like the rush of a violent wind, and it filled the entire house where they were sitting ... All of them were filled with the Holy Spirit and began to speak in other languages, as the Spirit gave them ability.

— Acts 2:2-4

Here is a statement by Elie Wiesel that I came across. "Words can sometimes in moments of grace, attain to the quality of deeds." I do believe that is so. I also believe it true to say that in moments of gracelessness words also attain the quality of deeds. In fact, I believe that words are deeds that can hurt or heal, divide or unite, tear down or build up.

To assign such significance to words flies in the face of much in our upbringing, culture, and experience that predisposes us to devalue the power of words. Maybe it is those old sayings we learned early on: "silence is golden"; "one picture is worth a thousand words"; "actions speak louder than words." Maybe it is the times when we were admonished as children to hush up, button our lips, or to mind our tongues. Or maybe we recall the nicknames given to some of our companions: loud mouth, big mouth, motor mouth.

There is something in our culture that leads us to devalue words. Readers of Marshall McCluhan in the '60s got the message that words are dead. Eliza Doolittle in *My Fair Lady* sang out, "Words, words, words, I'm so sick of words." A few years ago, Madonna had a hit song, "Papa Don't Preach." There is also much in our national experience that makes words suspect. Words from high places have been used to deceive, cover up, and stonewall.

Yet here is the strange thing. Despite the influences that would devalue words, the closing years of this century have become quite noisy. Talk radio has birthed a host of strident and angry voices. Rap music has become a significant part of the verbal cacophony. Questions about the influence of words are resurfacing in our midst. Are words dead? Or do words just begin to live once they leave our lips?

In this twentieth century we have certainly had examples of the way words carry an influence that can stir the winds. Think of Adolf Hitler whose words mesmerized his listeners and seduced them with a vision of power and superiority. Think of Winston Churchill whose words sustained not only the English but also the people of Nazi-occupied Europe who covertly tuned their radios to the British Broadcasting Company. It was said of Churchill, "He mobilized the English language and sent it into battle." Think of Martin Luther King whose words renewed the vision of a fairer and more just society.

Draw a smaller circle and think of the words we speak every day and the influence of those words upon others. Think of words that can hurt and wound others. In Greek the word for flesh is *sarx*. The Roman charioteer wielded a sharp whip that cut into the flesh, the sarx, of his horse. There is the origin of our English word *sarcasm*. There are cutting words that can wound our sensibilities. The psalmist speaks of "those who whet their tongues like swords, who aim bitter words like arrows" (Psalm 64:3).

The late Gordon W. Alport of Harvard in his monumental book, *The Nature of Prejudice*, described the context of genocide in terms of a pyramid. The word for genocide current today is ethnic cleansing. Think of a pyramid with different layers. At the apex of the pyramid is genocide. The supporting layer is persecution. Persecution emerges out of discrimination, which is the next layer down. The bottom layer, which provides the base for the whole pyramid, Alport called circumlocution. By that he meant all the words of prejudice, stereotype, and dehumanization that circulate throughout the whole society, in each little circle that makes up that whole. Out of memory come these words. "Boys flying kites haul in their winged birds. You can't do that when you are flying words." Words travel far and have a cumulative social impact. The writer of the letter to the Ephesians makes an intriguing reference to the Evil One as "the ruler of the atmosphere."

Words can also heal and bind up. Think of some time when you were down in the dumps and someone's word to you at just the right time became an enabling word. Think of the time when a kind word of yours to another person evoked the response, "You have just made my day."

Words, words, words! Words that hurt and words that heal. Words that set person against person, group against group. Words that disrupt community and words that create community. You and I have a central concern with words, for in the kingdom enterprise we traffic in words. The imperatives of our Lord involve us in the use of words. The Word, capital W, is central to our experience. "The Word, the Word, I say, is the bearer of grace." Luther said that. We are called to be messengers of the grace-laden Word.

Here is an observation worth noting. Ezekiel's vision of the valley of dry bones and Luke's of the day of Pentecost have some intriguing similarities. Both Ezekiel and Luke are witnessing to the mystery of God's creative action in history. In both accounts we meet a configuration of the words wind, breath, and spirit. How do you describe the creative action of God in our human experience? Can it all be wrapped up in a neat verbal package? Can our human vocabulary bear the weight of a reality that transcends our powers of precise definition? Do we not have to rely on metaphors, especially when dealing with the mystery of God?

Wind, breath, spirit: these words are interchangeable in biblical metaphor for the creative action of God. Listen to the writer of Genesis. "In the beginning when God created the heavens and the earth, the earth was formless and void and darkness covered the face of the deep, while a wind from God spread over the face of the deep" (Genesis 1:1). Then God speaks and his Word brings into being things that are not. The Word is central.

Listen to Ezekiel bringing the word from beyond to the living dead. "Come from the four winds, O breath, and breathe upon these slain, that they may live." What a beautiful way to speak of the Divine Spirit that animates the whole creation! Mark the configuration of wind, breath, and word also in Luke's account. Wind, spirit, and speech are woven into the artistry of Luke. How else do you express a reality that grabs us in a way we cannot define but can affirm? And what is the bottom line in both accounts? Just this — the recreation of community. Relationship is what it is all about, life in relationship to the Living God and to one another, to the Living God as made known to us in the Living Word, our crucified and risen Lord.

I can never read chapter 37 of Ezekiel without thinking of the words of the old spiritual. "The toe bone connected to the foot bone, the foot bone connected to the shin bone, the shin bone connected to the knee bone, the knee bone connected to the thigh bone, the thigh bone connected to the hip bone, the hip bone connected to the back bone, the back bone connected to the head bone, ain't it a wonder how them bones connected up!" Well, the human body with its manifold connections is a wonder. But bones, sinews, flesh, blood, organs, and brain do not a whole person make. That's what the prophet says in his unique way, "But there was no breath in them" — no life, no spirit — connections without either communion or community. The word zombies comes to mind, the living dead.

There is more to being human than just being a collection of bones, tissue, organs, and blood encased in flesh. "Prophesy to the breath, mortal, and say to the breath: Thus says the Lord God: Come from the four winds, O breath, and breathe upon these slain that they may live." The prophet invokes the mysterious, animating spirit of the whole of creation. And hear what happens. "I prophesied as he commanded me, and the breath came into them, and they lived, and stood on their feet, a vast multitude." Mark carefully the yoking of speech and spirit. Here is the affirmation being voiced. The biblical phrase, to stand before God, means to assume our fully human posture. This is the language of relationship. This is what Pentecost is all about, living in relationship with God and with one another, and our crucified and risen Lord defines for us the nature of those relationships. Individual and collective arrogance is out; redemptive concern for one another is in. This theme of inclusive community is especially prominent in Luke`s account of Pentecost.

Think about it this way. In the time of Jesus, holiness meant ritual purity. To be holy was to be superior to others. That way of saying "holy" is still around. The movements of racial superiority and ethnic purity still much in evidence in our world are other ways of saying, "We are holier than you." Class snobbery is a way of saying "holier than you." Elitism of any sort is a way of saying "holier than you." Religious posturing and fanatacism of any ilk is a way of saying, "holier than you."

But this is not what Jesus meant by holiness. This is not what Luke meant when proclaiming the Holy Spirit. Here are some words from an English scholar that will be helpful to us. "But because of its newly established close association with Jesus, the idea of holiness suffered a revolution in meaning. Instead of denoting ritual separation from defilement, it came to denote that intense dedication to the mercy and compassion of God which had led Jesus to touch lepers and fraternize with the more unsavory members of the community. Holiness was turned inside out: instead of meaning 'holier than thou,' it meant 'dedicated for thee.' And it was the Holy Spirit that gave to Christians that 'sanctification' or dedication that enabled them to follow in the steps of a holiness of this worldly and world-affirming sort."[1]

So, we are back where we began with the configuration of wind, word, spirit, and community. There are mean-spirited words that can stir the ill winds that fragment community. There are redemptive words of hope and promise that can heal, build up, and include. We are called to be messengers, to traffic in words, to speak words that attain to the level of grace. I do not mean the self-consciously pious kind of words. I do not mean the "Hey, friend, are you saved?" sort of words. I mean words that build mutual respect, words that engender a vision of community, words that appeal to conscience, words that call us to be all that we can be — words that will be bearers of the Word that is the very breath of life.

---

1. Moule, C.F.D., *The Holy Spirit,* William B. Eerdmans Publishing Company, Grand Rapids, Michigan, 1978, p. 23.

Isaiah 6:1-8   Holy Trinity

R.S.V.P.

Whom shall I send, and who will go for us?
                                                 —Isaiah 6:8b

    Sometimes it is interesting to take a biblical passage and just go through it line by line, letting the sparks fly out. This is the way I have opted to deal with today's first reading. Isaiah is one of the prophets who has given us an account of a turning point experience in his life. Some of his imagery will seem strange to us. But if we can get behind it there is something powerful here to which we can relate as well as a piercing word to us in the here and now.
    Listen! Isaiah begins: "In the year that King Uzziah died." That is the date of his experience. That year is 735 B.C. That is the date. But saying it the way he does the prophet gives us much more than a date. Uzziah had leprosy and a regent ruled in his stead. The prevailing piety regarded leprosy as a sign of the disfavor of God. The writer of Chronicles said Uzziah was made a leper because he had usurped priestly perogatives. The writer of Kings said it was because Uzziah tolerated the shrines and high places where the practice of magic and sacred prostitution compromised the faith of Israel. So Isaiah's way of dating tells us that this was an ominous time in the nation's history. The leper king

was dead and the battalions of the predatory Assyrians were on the march, edging ever closer to Palestine.

Fear and foreboding were in the air. The prophet felt the chill of anxiety in his bones. External changes were triggering an inner crisis in Isaiah's life. We can relate to that. We really cannot separate what goes on around us from what goes on within us.

It was in such an uncertain time of change and threat that Isaiah tells us, "I saw the Lord sitting on a throne, high and lofty." He experienced a moment of perception, of new awareness. That's what biblical writers are trying to express when they use this kind of language. In the biblical sense, seeing is perceiving. Jesus often chided his disciples for having eyes but seeing not, ears but hearing not.

Some may have difficulty with the word *throne* here. There is a disposition abroad that shies away from words like *king, Lord,* and *master* as not appropriate in this day and age. Isaiah's vision of the Lord upon a throne high and lofty remains. What he seeks to share with us here is a sense of the complete otherness of the Sovereign God. What he seeks to communicate is a sense of a transcendent order of reality. And this is precisely what has gone into eclipse in our urban culture in this century.

Someone has said the mission of the church is to keep alive the rumor that there is a God: a God who sees, and knows, and cares, and judges. With the eclipse of a sense of the transcendent in our culture has come the absence of a sense of personal and collective accountability. The cry "mea culpa!" seems to belong to yesterday. Today we make mistakes in judgment. I recall being in a courtroom as the judge sentenced a man who while drunk had shot and wounded a man. Standing in the dock the convicted man looked at the wounded man, who was present, and said, "I'm sorry." Good grief, that's what you say when you inadvertently step on someone's toe or bump into him. Whatever happened to the anguished prayer of the publican, "O God, be merciful to me, a sinner"? Whatever happened to the cry of the returning son, "Father, I have sinned against heaven and before you"?

What has gone into eclipse is precisely what Isaiah recovered as he came alive to transcendent mystery of the holy God before whom we along with the angels stand vulnerable and from whose gaze we seek to shield our nakedness. The seraphs hid themselves behind their wings. We do it with excuses and blame. Ours has been called a nation of victims, a culture of blame. That's the insight behind the imagery of the seraphs who shield with their wings their nakedness before the high and holy God. Remember Isaiah is trying to give expression to a mystery that cannot be fully grasped by our human vocabulary.

Needless to say, the God Isaiah perceives is not *The Man Upstairs*. Isaiah's language does not convey the image of a homespun good old boy with whom we can lounge around the cracker barrel for chit-chat. This is not some little domesticated god of our own making. If I could carry a tune, I would burst out singing the words that Walter C. Smith composed and set to the old Welsh Melody, St. Denio.

> *Immortal, invisible, God only wise,*
> *In light inaccessible hid from our eyes,*
> *Most blessed, most glorious, the Ancient of Days,*
> *Almighty, victorious, thy great name we praise.*

The language of praise, mystery, and wonder is more appropriate to our approach to God. And Isaiah used these words to express the heart of his vision of God. "But the Lord of hosts is exalted by justice, and the Holy God shows himself holy by righteousness" (Isaiah 5:16).

Isaiah's response to his vision is utter speechlessness. I know that the New Revised Standard Version translates his response as "Woe is me, I am lost." Some argue for another translation, "Woe is me, I am struck dumb." This seems more reasonable in the light of the rest of Isaiah's statement, "For I am a man of unclean lips and I live among a people of unclean lips; yet my eyes have seen the King, the Lord of hosts!" In the blinding light of God's holiness what do any of us have to say in our own defense? We make judgmental assessments about one another and measure one another by degrees of difference. But before the blinding light of the Holy God do not the differences between us get dwarfed into insignificance and the similarities stand out? Does not the evil we see outwardly displayed in others exist also in us as a hidden darkness?

The prophet's confession of unclean lips catches our attention. We think of the ritual uncleanness of the leper king, Uzziah. The confession suggests an uncleanness of language, an impurity of speech, pollution and contamination in our very hearts where our thoughts and values shape the words that come forth from our lips. "Out of the abundance of the heart the mouth speaks." Jesus said that.

Here is a thought to roll around in your head. When we lose a sense of the transcendent God, we also lose a vision of our own humanity. The human dimension goes into eclipse and this is reflected in many ways. The marketing-inspired image of the person as consumer diminishes us. Pornography dehumanizes our personhood. The adulation of the lifestyles of the rich and famous proclaims an inadequate message about what it means to be a successful human being. Indifference to the claims of Divine justice and righteousness triggers social dislocations and chaos.

"Yet!" "Yet!" What a crucial little word Isaiah inserts in his account. It reminds us of the crucial little "But now" that Paul shouts out in the third chapter of his letter to the church in Rome at the end of his diagnosis of our human condition. Hear again that confession of Isaiah with its remarkable conclusion. "Woe is me! I am lost, for I am a man of unclean lips, and I live among a people of unclean lips; yet my eyes have seen the King, the Lord of hosts!" Here is the wondrous thing! God wills to disclose himself to us!

God wills to reach out and touch the life of Isaiah. God wills to disclose himself to us! That is the meaning behind the powerful imagery of the seraph who touches the prophet's lips with a burning coal. H. G. Wells is reported to have said, "I cannot believe that whoever is up there would reach down and shake hands with me." The story is told of a little boy who didn't quite understand the words of the Lord's prayer. His parents overheard him one night saying his prayers before bedtime. "Our Father, who art in New Haven, how do you know my name?" That is a good question. Think of the Lord of all creation and the mystery boggles the mind. Yet it is the central and wondrous affirmation of the faith. It was to this God, high and lofty, to whom Jesus prayed with the simple and intimate word of the Aramaic household, *Abba*, the equivalent of our English word *Daddy*. Set aside any discomfort with masculine language here for the sake of hearing the mind-boggling proclamation of the high and lofty God who is so far and yet so near!

So Isaiah has seen the Lord, high and lofty. He has seen himself and his community in a new way and a flash of humbling insight. Now he hears what his ears had not heard before. He hears the pathos of God. "Then I heard the voice of the Lord saying, 'Whom shall I send, and who will go for us?'" This passage has traditionally been identified as Isaiah's call to ministry. But there is no direct call. No voice thunders out, "Isaiah, I have chosen you for a special task." Isaiah just hears. He has become a listener and what he hears moves him to a response, "Here am I; send me!"

Our gospel reading today introduces us to John's unique way of speaking about the lifting up of Jesus. His whole gospel is an invitation to see the Lord, high and lifted up, and to hear the voice from on high. And doesn't each gospel in its own way bid us to hear the pathos of God in the cries of the oppressed, the sighs of the sorrowing, the weeping of the little ones, the appeals of the excluded? In and through our crucified and Risen Lord, do we not hear the question posed for us, "Whom shall I send and who will go for us?"

1 Samuel 3:1-10 (11-20) Proper 4
Pentecost 2
Corpus Christi

Here Is Where It Happens

Here is where it happens. Where is here? Here is right here, among us. Here is the community of faith, and every local congregation, large or small, is a visible manifestation of that community. The gathered community of faith is the port of entry for the initiatives of God. That is the it, the initiative of God. Does saying that place too high an estimation upon the local congregation?

If your answer is yes, then think about this. The storytellers of the Bible preface pivotal events with scenes that are domestic, institutional and familiar to all of us. What can be more familiar to us than hearth and altar, family and local church? Here is where each of us begins our pilgrimage with God from baptism to confirmation to mission and discipleship. Here is where faith is nurtured and sustained week after week after week. Here is where the lamp of God is tended, however faintly at times it seems to burn. Do not devalue the family and the local congregation, our extended family in Christ. As ordinary as home and shrine may appear, they are vital centers in the Divine/human encounter and dialogue.

Isn't that the sort of thing Luke was saying in his infancy narratives that focus on a fragile little family and wider community of faith and tradition represented by Zechariah, Elizabeth, Simeon,

Anna, and the teachers in the Temple? Try to tell Luke that hearth and altar are not vital centers where Divine initiatives happen, initiatives that will impact the future.

Recall today's first reading in which we meet the child Samuel serving in the shrine at Shiloh. In fact, some day take the time to compare the first two chapters of Luke's gospel with the first three chapters of 1 Samuel. Note the similarity of focus of hearth and altar, family and institution. Only in the first three chapters of 1 Samuel it is not Mary and Joseph that we meet, but Hannah and Elkanah. Hannah, like Mary, receives a child from God. Hannah, like Mary, sings in exultation. Eli received Samuel in the shrine as Simeon did Jesus. Think of the twelve-year-old Jesus among the teachers in the Temple and Samuel under the tutelage of Eli.

The similarities in the narratives are striking. And both narratives stand as prefaces to pivotal events. The story of Samuel's birth prefaces the history of the birth of a nation in which Samuel was a key actor. Luke's infancy narrative prefaces the birth of a new humanity in and through the ministry of Jesus.

In both narratives the bottom line for us is the community of faith as the port of entry for Divine initiatives. What we need to hear is a word about the importance of our trusteeship of the faith tradition in the institutional church, and the vital center of the church as institution is the local congregation. It is in the local church in a local community that the rubber hits the road.

It seems preposterous, doesn't it, to think that in this world filled with shadows and uncertainties, sound and fury, that what goes on in our little church circles can have any impact. We even have trouble believing that what goes on within our little congregations with all their imperfections can have any significant national influence. In a way we can sometimes be like Eli, sort of pooped out and unexpectant. We are told about things in general then that "the word of the Lord was rare in those days; visions were not widespread." The writer's comment about the failing eyesight of Eli is a way of saying that the spiritual bank was pretty much bankrupt.

But here's the writer's point: even in this faith community where the light of faith was waning, it was still flickering. The ever-creating God was about to bring something new into being. This is really a creation story. This isn't an Horatio Alger story about a boy who becomes a successful man. This story is a testimony to the God who calls us into existence and calls to us to enlist us in his service. He makes the barren rejoice and calls into being the things that are not. This story is a reminder to us of the God who calls us into being and in and through our life together calls to us. This is the real drama of life and history.

This story was put in its final shape and circulated three centuries after the birth of Samuel. It was written up in a day when the institutions of Israel had lost their credibility. The kings, captains, and priests had made a mess of the heritage bequeathed to them. Disenchantment was in the air. This story proclaims the possibilities of God even in the worst of times.

The story functions also as a critique. The call of God and his claim upon our hearts, mind, and conscience: these are the essentials for a tomorrow of God's own making. Soul, conscience, Spirit, the call of God: these are the raw materials for a tomorrow that has a chance of being something more than the repetition of the same old thing, a tomorrow of God's own making.

I turn at this point to the young people in our midst. This season of the year is also graduation time. We recognize our high school and college seniors who are graduating. We make plans for church school Sunday, distribute Bibles, and present awards. Your years of formal schooling have sought to equip you with skills for tomorrow. And how important that is for you in a world undergoing rapid technological change. But how crucial to that world of tomorrow are the values, loyalties, and convictions that will guide your life. This is where church comes in.

I think here of a story about an old street-wise New York cat who managed to survive in the area around Columbus Circle. He was a veteran alley cat. One day a mouse escaped his claws and hid in a storm drain just under the curb of the sidewalk. The mouse was trembling but remained quiet, knowing the cat was probably waiting for him to exit. Suddenly the mouse heard a horrendous meow followed by an equally dreadful bark. Then there was silence. "Ha, ha," thought the mouse, "that old cat has finally had his comeuppance." After a few minutes, as the mouse cautiously inched forward out of the storm drain, a mean-looking paw suddenly grabbed him. As the cat held him and looked him in the eye, the mouse said, "I thought I heard a dog bark." "You did," said the cat, "but in order to survive in New York you've got to be bilingual!"

Dear friends, young and old and in between, the cat has the right of it. We've got to be bilingual to survive in the fullest and truest sense. We need the vocabulary of this world. We need also the words of the Spirit that warm the heart, inform the conscience, and enlighten the mind. We need the teaching that makes us smart. We need the Word from beyond that makes us wise. We need the skills that help us set up ledgers and accounts. We need also our faith tradition that calls us to be accountable. We need to know more than computer jargon and be familiar with more than the internet. What about the eternity network? Didn't Peter sense this in his own way when he exclaimed, "Lord, to whom can we go? You have the words of eternal life" (John 6:68).

I recall my own first days on the college campus. I remember sitting down with my assigned faculty advisor to discuss the choice of an elective course. I thought I would like to take an introductory course on New Testament studies. He shrugged and commented, "It might have some cultural value, but it would have no practical value." Then he went on to share these comments: "It's all a matter of the range of choices you want open to you in later life. Do you, for example, want to be in the position of having to choose between attending a concert or going to a ball game in any one week, or do you want to have enough money in order to do both? In other words, do you want enough money to extend your range of options?" There it was, a vision of tomorrow in terms of what this world has to offer. I confess to heeding his counsel and replaced the proposed elective with another.

But this was wartime and soon I was in the army. I suppose it was being exposed firsthand to the ruin and carnage that humans can inflict on one another that made me doubt my hasty assent to the pronouncement that the story of the man named Jesus had no practical value. In every direction one looked there was the cross. Maybe I was one of the blind being counseled and led by the blind.

So the doubt was sown and it was a good doubt. What happens in us and in our world when the transcendent claim of God goes into eclipse? What happens when intelligence is no longer informed by conscience? What happens when human relations are void of redemptive compassion — when life choices are based on inadequate definitions of what it means to be a man or a woman? Some doubts are good doubts.

Think again about the community of faith and those who in its midst have been birthed to go forth and make a difference on small stages and large stages. This where we hear God calling to us, calling us by name. This is where it happens — if we let it happen. Let these words from today's reading form our prayer, "Speak, Lord, for your servant is listening."

1 Samuel 8:4-20 (11:14-15)　　　　　　　　Proper 5
　　　　　　　　　　　　　　　　　　　　Pentecost 3
　　　　　　　　　　　　　　　　　　　Ordinary Time 10

Saul, The Tormented King

He was like a meteor. He blazed brightly and briefly across the skies of Israel before burning out and falling to the ground. You can sum up the life of the first king of Israel in just such words. The priests who wrote about him rejected him outright. But then, they had a special reason for doing that. Saul did not always see things their way. Most of the people he led followed him to the end. Perhaps theirs is the better testimony.

You will find Saul's story in the first book of Samuel. It is quite a readable book containing thirty-one fast-paced chapters. It is also a baffling book. There are repetitions and contradictions. Those occur because 1 Samuel is not the work of just one writer. The editors have woven together at least two sources that cover the same period of history. Each source has its own unique outlook. One source, the earlier, looked upon the monarchy in Israel as a fine thing. These writers may well have been part of the royal court in the days of Solomon. The second source takes a rather dim view of kings. Both points of view shine forth in today's reading. It's as if one blended together two interpretations of American history, one favoring states rights and the other favoring a strong central government. In 1 Samuel the editors just blended both interpretations. Scholars consider the earlier view that takes an optimistic view of monarchy as not only more accurate as history, but more skillfully written.

It is not too difficult to accept the view of the earlier source that some form of unification was necessary if the twelve separate tribes were ever to achieve security in their new land. A king and a national army were essential. The people reached that conclusion after a major Philistine victory at the battle of Ebenezer. Who was it in our early history who warned, "If we do not hang together, we shall all hang separately"? As far as the people in ancient Israel were concerned, the question was no longer "shall we have a king" but "who shall be our king."

At this point Saul enters biblical history. He comes out of obscurity. When we first meet him he is not politicking for the crown. He is out looking for some lost asses and about to give up the search when one of his servants suggests they consult Samuel. The child priest we met last week has become the eminent priestly leader with more than local reputation and influence. The minute his eyes fell on the handsome and striking Saul, Samuel knew he had found the one to be first king of Israel. He entertained Saul in lavish fashion. They dined together on the roof of Samuel's house in full public view, an adroit way of letting everyone know that this handsome fellow had found favor in the eyes of the priest. Samuel even managed to find the lost asses of Saul. Saul must have been both impressed and dazzled. But if that was not enough, before he left Samuel anointed him with oil, an action that proclaimed Saul as God's chosen leader.

Not everyone applauded the choice of Saul. The drums of discord were beating. But an occasion to test the leadership of Saul soon presented itself. One of the vulnerable border cities in the Trans-Jordan, Jabesh-gilead, was besieged by the Ammonites. The citizens sued for peace. Nahash, the Ammonite king, announced that the price of peace would be the gouging of the right eye of every male citizen. That was a cruel and needless demand intended to humiliate the city. Nahash gave them a seven day grace period to reflect. The people of Jabesh-gilead sent word to Samuel, who summoned Saul.

We are told that when Saul heard the news the spirit of God came upon him mightily. Saul cut up a yoke of oxen and sent the pieces throughout the tribes, both as a challenge and as a warning of the price of refusal. The volunteers came from all the tribes. The Ammonites were soundly defeated and Saul earned the lasting gratitude of the people of the liberated city. The people of Jabesh-gilead asked Samuel to point out those who opposed the selection of Saul. "Give them to us that we may put them to death." Saul restrained them, was crowned at a tribal gathering at Gilgal, and as his first act established a standing army of three thousand soldiers. His kingship would be no easy task. His reign would never know a day free from war, death, or harassment of one sort or another. Some things would go right. Many things would go wrong. From the start, dark clouds hung over his reign.

Relations with Samuel would have much to do with Saul's life. He revered Samuel almost to the point of making an idol of him. Yet Samuel was autocratic and often severe in his religious outlook. One day, for example, when people had come from far and wide for a ceremony at Gilgal, Samuel was late in arriving and people began to drift away. Saul, afraid they would all leave, took it upon himself to preside over the burnt offering. Samuel was infuriated by this assumption of the priestly role. In a fit of anger he announced to Saul the end of his reign, "The Lord has picked out a new man after his own heart." Did the flinty Samuel confuse his own voice with the voice of God? Clergy sometimes do, but big egos can be encountered in any vocation.

The final breach with Samuel came when he ordered Saul to undertake a revenge expedition against a Bedouin tribe called the Amalekites and settle some old scores. Samuel invoked the *harem* which means the *ban*, a term that applied to a holy war. The enemy people were to be destroyed along with their livestock and property. Holy wars linger on our planet. Before we call Samuel's order an example of ancient savagery, we want to remember that in this century all nations have participated in turning civilian populations into targets.

The whole incident left a scar inside Saul. Samuel, after all, represented the voice of God in Israel. Saul became broody, guilt-ridden, ill tempered. "The Spirit of the Lord departed from him and an evil spirit entered him." That is the primitive diagnosis of the writers. Saul became uneasy, suspicious, despondent, given to outbursts of temper. Yet he had reasons. He could not help but know that Samuel was making a covert search for another king. He found that future king, a young man named David.

We all have Sunday school memories of the young David who was taken into the entourage of Saul to calm the troubled king by playing the lyre and serving as his armor-bearer. We remember also the story of David's slaying of Goliath with a sling shot. While there is some doubt as to just who slayed Goliath, David is credited in this carefully embroidered account. David eventually became a captain in Saul's army and performed with exceptional success. One day the broody Saul heard some maidens singing in the street. "Saul has slain his thousands and David his ten thousands." Saul's jealousy and fear compounded. He felt threatened, not unlike a modern day older executive might feel uneasy as sharp, younger executives come into the company. Saul's state of mind was such that David's life was endangered. David fled to Judah, where he gathered a small army and, as an ancient Robin Hood preying on the Philistines, endeared himself to the common people under the Philistine heel.

Do we wonder why Saul became morose, anxiety ridden, a bit unbalanced? The task of building a unified nation out of twelve separate tribes was enormous. The well-armored Philistines were a constant threat. The breach with Samuel and the guerilla movement led by David was a daily thorn in his side. A sign of Saul's desperation is his visit to the witch of Endor to get a sign of things to come. Here is the king who should heed the Word from beyond consulting with a medium. When we are desperate, we are all vulnerable. The witch called up the ghost of Samuel, who as we might expect had no good word to speak to Saul. Saul's life is like an epic tragedy as an inexorable fate seems to close in upon him. At the battle of Gilboa, overpowered by the Philistine foe, his army defeated, his sons slain, Saul falls upon his own sword.

> *For God's sake, let us sit upon the ground*
> *And tell sad stories of the death of kings:*
> *How some have been depos'd; some slain in war;*
> *Some haunted by the ghosts they have deposed;*
> *Some poisoned by their wives; some sleeping killed;*
> *All murder'd: for within the hollow crown*
> *That rounds the mortal temples of a king*
> *Keeps death his court, and there the antic sits,*
> *Scoffing his state and grinning at his pomp,*
> *Allowing him a breath, a little scene,*
> *To monarchize, be feared, and kill with looks,*
> *Infusing him with self and vain conceit,*
> *As if this flesh which walls about our life*
> *Were brass impregnable; and humored thus*
> *Comes at the last and with a little pin*
> *Bores through his castle wall, and — farewell king!*
>   (Shakespeare, *King Richard II*, Act 3, Scene 2)

Farewell, king. Farewell, Saul. The Philistines cut off his head and sent it throughout their towns. They hung his body on the walls of Bethshan. It disappeared within 24 hours. The men of Jabesh-gilead (remember them?) risked their lives to retrieve it, a final and most meaningful tribute.

So, 1 Samuel gives us a portrait of the first king of Israel. He is not a knight in shining armor, a fellow always on top of everything. He is a very human person, a mix of victories and defeats, joy and sorrow. Saul is like us in our humanness. He lives, hurts, breathes, makes mistakes, suffers from his liabilities, cries, laughs, and gets angry. He is a mirror of ourselves.

Saul, in deep anguish and distress, withered under the flinty stare of Samuel. Parents continued to name their children after him. A thousand years later a baby lovingly named Saul, of the tribe of Benjamin as his namesake, was born in Tarsus in Asia Minor. He too would break under a load. But he saw something Saul did not see: not the flinty face of Samuel, but the glory of God in the face of Jesus Christ, and along with that vision came mercy, renewal, and a second chance. We know him as the apostle Paul.

1 Samuel 15:34—16:13   Proper 6
Pentecost 4
Ordinary Time 11

When Saints Go Marching Forth

Sometimes when reading you come across words that just leap off the page and grab you. Here is a comment by C.S. Lewis I encountered in his book, *Reflections On The Psalms*.

> *If the Divine call does not make us better, it will make us much worse. Of all bad people, religious bad people are the worst. Of all created beings the wickedest are those who originally stood in the presence of God.*

Let these words hover over our thoughts this morning. They are not comfortable words, for they remind us of some dark chapters in the history of the church, like the crusades, the inquisition, and the execution of witches. They are not comforting for they make us think about the religious fanatacism abroad in our own time. They are not comfortable, for they warn us of the pitfalls in our own spiritual pilgrimage. Keep them in mind.

We are with Samuel again this morning. The child acolyte in the shrine at Shiloh has become a king maker, a shaker and mover in Israel. He has done a tremendous job in forging a nation out of a loose confederation of tribes. The child called by God is now the respected spiritual leader of an infant nation. His words are heeded as the words of God. The little acolyte has come a long way.

How carefully did you listen to the first reading today? Samuel is out looking for another king to succeed Saul. There has been a painful parting of the ways between Saul and Samuel. "Then Samuel went to Ramah; and Saul went up to his house in Gibeah of Saul. Samuel did not see Saul again until the day of his death, but Samuel grieved over Saul. And the Lord was sorry that he had made Saul king over Israel."

Now, what is that all about? Well, it's a sad story and it's told in chapter 15 of 1 Samuel. I can understand why the lectionary sequence for this cycle just jumps over it. It raises questions we are content to gloss over. But we really dare not, for it is an example of the extent to which religious muscle flexing can go. Here is a case where we have to place the written word under the judgment of the Living Word.

The breach between Saul and Samuel came about in this way. Samuel, speaking in the name of God, commands Saul to attack and thoroughly destroy the Amalekites, "man and woman, child and infant, ox and sheep, camel and donkey." It is pay back time. The Amalekites were the people who resisted the advance of the Israelites out of Egypt.

Saul took his army and did as Samuel had ordered. But he did not destroy the healthy animals, nor the valuable property, nor the Amelekite king, Agag. Samuel was furious and went into a rage. He accused Saul of disobedience, told him he was washed up as king, and proceeded to hack Agag in pieces with a sword.

That is a bloody story. We shudder at the dimensions of the carnage Samuel insists upon in the name of God. But then the justifications for the doctrine of total war and the mass killing of civilian populations are not just some ancient aberration. Nor are we strangers to the way zeal of any sort can get mixed up with spiritual arrogance and ego to become zealotry.

Christian tradition has regarded Samuel, who acted as priest, prophet, and king, as a forerunner of Jesus. Samuel at this point in his life seems more like a forerunner of Torquemada, the grand inquisitor of the Inquisition. The writer of the New Testament epistle to the Hebrews gives us a portrait of Jesus as our High Priest. But Jesus, our High Priest, came not with a sword in his hand but a spear in his side.

But let's get out of yesterday and into today. What about the way arrogance and mean-spiritedness can get mixed up with the faith today? What about religious leaders who would be the makers and unmakers not of kings but of presidents, senators, and members of Congress? What about religious leaders in any time and place who go forth in the name of God as if to a holy war? There is a kind of religious triumphalism abroad in our land.

This is a different sort of religious activism. Advocacy on behalf of the poor and oppressed is not the agenda. Political control and power is the agenda. "The question is not who we will endorse (for president) but who will endorse our agenda."[1] That is the rhetoric of the new triumphalism. The words of Saint Paul directed at the zealotry of which he at one time had been a partisan come to mind. "I can testify that they have a zeal for God, but it is not enlightened" (Romans 10:2).

It is important that we recognize zealotry. It is also crucial that we recognize the potential for zealotry within ourselves. This is a danger for all who have strong convictions. There are times when we are not above heaping coals of fire upon the heads of those who do not share our convictions. Browse through the Psalms and note the way many of them boil over with self-righteous indignation and cries for vengeance.

Within the congregation of a pastor friend in another time and place there was a noted lay theologian. One day I commented to my friend, "What a wonderful help he must be in the ministry of your congregation." "Actually no," replied my colleague. "When he speaks up in church meetings, he says all the right things in all the wrong ways." The point here is that being in the right does not make us righteous. There are subtle ways that our egos can subvert our servanthood.

Our reading suggests that God was sorry he made Saul king and repented of the choice. That seems to suggest that God can make mistakes. The writers of 1 Samuel may have had a special interest in investing the king with Divine patronage. Saul, in all his inner torment, went on being king until the day he died. I would suggest putting it another way. God takes chances. He gambles not only on Saul and Samuel but on all of us. We live before him like these folk in biblical narratives, a mix of wings and warts. He calls all of us to be saints, to live lives rooted in God, sustained by God, and directed toward God. He gathers us together as a community of faith and sends us forth into the world. In going forth watch out for the pitfalls.

In what spirit shall we go forth? Here out of our book of worship are some beautiful words of commissioning.

> *Go forth into the world to serve God with gladness; be of good courage; hold fast to that which is good; render to no one evil for evil; strengthen the fainthearted; support the weak; help the afflicted; honor all people; love and serve God, rejoicing in the power of the Holy Spirit.*

Here are guidelines for our going forth.

---

1. A statement by the executive director of the Christian Coalition, Ralph Reed, reported by David Broder in an article, "The Christian Right Flexes Its Muscles," in the National Weekly Edition of the *Washington Post*, September, 18-24, 1995, p. 13.

1 Samuel 17:57—18:5,10-16   Proper 7
Pentecost 5
Ordinary Time 12

Acquaintances Or Friends?

Let's begin by thinking about the difference between an acquaintance and a friend. There is a difference. That difference is the dimension of depth. There are those who make the acquaintance of many and count that as social success. So, one can end up with many acquaintances but no real friends, for a friend is much more than an acquaintance. The proverbial wisdom of Israel made the distinction this way. "Some friends play at friendship, but a true friend sticks closer than one's nearest kin" (Proverbs 18:24). This poses a question to us. If you want to make a finger count of your acquaintances, would ten fingers be enough? Hardly! If you want to count your friends, are ten fingers more than enough?

In the biblical narratives there are two stories of friendship that stand out. One is the story of Naomi and her daughter-in-law, Ruth, who stayed by her side through thick and thin. The other is the friendship whose beginning is highlighted in today's first reading, the bonding of Jonathan and David.

You are certainly familiar with David. You may not be as knowledgeable about Jonathan, the eldest son of the tormented first king of Israel, Saul. He is worth knowing. Reflect on his story and a configuration of adjectives will come to mind: generous, gallant, loyal, sympathetic, valiant, magnanimous. Jonathan can be described in all those ways and more.

Jonathan enters the biblical narrative in 1 Samuel 14 and there you will meet him serving on the field of battle in his father's army. Jonathan and his armor bearer take a strategic action that wins the day. When the battle is over Jonathan comes upon a honeycomb and takes a taste that at once energizes him and creates a problem for him. The troops inform him that Saul has issued an order forbidding the troops to eat anything before sundown. Saul's head was filled with all sorts of religious quirks. Jonathan is nonplussed and states in public his disagreement, "My father has troubled the land."

Meanwhile, Saul is trying to get some advice from God about the next step in the campaign. When he can't get through to God he concludes that somehow sin has gotten into the picture. He announces that whoever is responsible will die, even if it is his own son. Through the casting of lots the finger points directly to Jonathan, who confesses that he took a taste of honey. Saul vows to kill him but the people rise as one and bluntly tell the king not to touch one hair of Jonathan's head. The common soldiers sensed than Jonathan was a peoples' person.

Jonathan's next appearance in the narrative is in today's reading. David is introduced to Saul. As far as Jonathan was concerned, meeting David was a case of friendship at first sight. "When David had finished speaking to Saul, the soul of Jonathan was bound to the soul of David, and Jonathan loved him as his own soul ... Then Jonathan made a covenant with David because he loved him as his own soul." To confirm his covenant Jonathan did a startling and significant thing. "Jonathan stripped himself of the robe that he was wearing, and gave it to David, and his armor, and even his sword and his bow and his belt." What a way to recognize another as one's alter ego, a trusted friend, a soul mate! And what unparalleled generosity, for this action invests David with heirship to the throne.

The guilelessness of Jonathan hits us as we reflect that he had nothing to gain. This is not a calculated action, for David is a potential rival for the throne of Israel. No ego is involved as in the failed relationship of Saul and Samuel. No jealousy is present as in the stormy love/hate relationship that would develop between Saul and David. And if you read on in this narrative you will see the rare kind of friend that Jonathan was to David while yet remaining loyal to his father and finally dying beside him on the field of battle. David was devastated when he heard that news.

> *How the mighty have fallen*
> *in the midst of the battle!*
> *Jonathan lies slain upon your high places.*
> *I am distressed for you, my brother Jonathan*
> *greatly beloved were you to me;*
> *your love to me was wonderful,*
> *passing the love of women.*
> — 2 Samuel 2:25-26

These were part of the words of tribute composed by David.

But a question about this friendship emerges. Would it have lasted? This is after all a friendship between two young people. It has been compared to the friendship of Damon and Pythias, the Greek philosophers, and to the friendship of Roland and Oliver in the *Song of Roland*. But none of these friendships are long term friendships. Could this friendship of Jonathan and David have survived the passage of time and the punishment David meted out to some of the entourage of Saul?

Think back to some of the friendships of your own youth and the seriousness with which you invested them. Go through the pages of your high school year book and ponder them as you look at the pictures and read the autographed comments. Have those friendships survived the passage of time and the realities of adulthood? Of course, in our mobile society we move away from others geographically. But there are other ways to move away from one another.

The play, *Inherit The Wind*, revolves around the Scopes trial and the argument between the opposing attorneys, William Jennings Bryan and Clarence Darrow. During the play Matthew Brady (Bryan) says to Henry Drummond (Darrow), "What happened?

We used to be friends. Why have we drifted apart?" Drummond replies, "All motion is relative, perhaps it is you who have drifted away by standing still."

That can and does happen. Friendship is best nurtured through ongoing conversation and dialogue. That does not mean we cannot have differences of opinion with a friend. On the contrary, it is only with a friend that you can have a worthwhile debate. It is the mutual covenant of acceptance, love, and trust that frees us for genuine exchange. Sydney Harris, who for many years wrote a daily column for the Chicago *Daily News*, was right on the button when he commented one day: "Strangers can only be polite; it requires friends to quarrel. When strangers have an argument about politics, religion, or art, they are but defending their personality rather than their point of view. Two friends can come to grips with the subject honestly and rudely. This is why so many social arguments are fruitless and shallow. Each contestant is secretly trying to prove his or her supremacy to the other; logic and reason are only incidental weapons."

The quality of our relationships can be judged by the depth of our conversation. Gabbling and gossiping and idle conversation are the hallmark of superficial friendship. Someone has argued that the game of bridge functions as a way for us to be with others in a way that ensures shallowness to conversation. The proverb makers of Israel spoke of playing at friendship. Here is a well-taken translation of the text from Proverbs quoted earlier. "There is a companion who does nothing but chatter, but there is a friend who sticks closer than kin."[1]

Speaking of chatter reminds me of the tourist who tried to strike up a conversation with a taciturn fisherman in Down East Maine. "You folks do not talk very much do you?" asked the tourist. "Nope," replied the fisherman, "only when it improves on the silence." Silence, incidentally, is something we can best share with a friend. It is said that Ralph Waldo Emerson and Henry David Thoreau could spend hours together, the silence broken only by an occasional request, "Pass the baccy."

We have thought together about the distinction between an acquaintance and a friend. We have recalled the covenant of friendship between Jonathan and David. We have shared some thoughts about the depth dimension of real friendship. Now, the inevitable question presents itself. What kinds of friends are we to him who has made with us a covenant of friendship? "I do not call you servants any longer, because the servant does not know what the master is doing; but I have called you friends, because I have made known to you everything that I have heard from my Father" (John 15:15).

"What a friend we have in Jesus," so we sing. But ask this, what kind of friends does Jesus have in us? Are we friends or are we just casual acquaintances? Do we nourish this relationship by interacting with his words? Do we sustain it through prayer, silent or spoken? Are we there for him the way he is and always will be for us? "What a friend we have in Jesus, all our cares and griefs to bear." Do we share the griefs that weighed upon him? Do we share the imperatives that sent him into a ministry of compassion and conviction?

Each gospel writer in his own way tells us that friendship with God is not a possibility bound by either geography or time. The gospel writers can introduce us to Jesus of Nazareth. Whether or not we just remain nodding acquaintances or dependable friends is up to us.

---

1. McKane, William. *Proverbs*. Westminster Press. Philadelphia. 1975

2 Samuel 1:1, 17-27

Proper 8
Pentecost 6
Ordinary Time 13

Lyrics For The Centuries

When David received the report of the battlefield deaths of Saul and Jonathan, he expressed his sorrow and tribute by composing and chanting a lament, that beautiful elegy that is today's first reading. A line from an old spiritual comes to mind. "Little David, play on your harp." Yes, David, play and sing for us the lyrics that span the centuries. Sing the songs that help us express our mourning while celebrating the lives of those whose loss we mourn. Sing us the songs that sustain us when we are beset by ills and those that buoy us in the struggle for justice and peace. Give us the canticles to express praise and thanksgiving and the poetry of confession. David, take up your harp for us.

Think of David and what picture comes to mind? My guess is the picture inherited from early days in church school, that of the shepherd boy downing Goliath with a slingshot, the warrior lad who became the king of Israel. Today, I invite you to think of him as a musician, composer, and minstrel. David was a singer of songs. His songs are part of our spiritual heritage. Some musicians come along and their music speaks to a particular decade. The lyrics of David span the centuries. David is the patron of the great music of the faith. His battles are part of the dust of history. His lyrics endure and forever surface in our liturgy.

In Joseph Heller's comic novel, *God Knows*, David tells his story. At one point he has this to say as he compares himself to Moses. "Moses has the Ten Commandments, it's true, but I've got much better lines. I've got the poetry and passion, savage violence and the plain raw civilizing grief of human heartbreak. 'The beauty of Israel is slain upon the high places.' That sentence is mine and so is 'They were swifter than eagles, they were stronger than lions. My psalms last.' "[1] David's psalms have indeed endured and we can with justification call him the patron of choral music in the community of faith.

As a small boy David probably learned to play the harp as a means of earning a livelihood. As the youngest son in a large family he would receive no inheritance. That went to the oldest son. David's talent probably suggested the vocation of minstrel. Such musicians not only entertained as they do today, they also accompanied the prophetic groups who danced ecstatically, like the proverbial whirling dervishes of the Middle East. When David entered the court of Saul, it was as a musician whose task was to soothe the tortured brow of Saul with harp and song. Music therapy is not new. How many of us find renewal in just listening to music that nourishes us?

Every age has its own background music that can stir, soothe, or even inflame. During our own civil war the "Battle Cry of Freedom" rallied Union troops while the "Bonny Blue Flag" stirred Confederate soldiers. Hitler's brown shirts marched into history inflamed by the music and lyrics of the Horst Wessel song. Think of the influence of the songs of Bob Dylan during the '60s or the confidence of those who struggled for human rights expressed in the song, "We Shall Overcome." The latter decades of this century have moved from soft rock to hard rock to acid rock and heavy metal to gangster rap. Every decade produces its own music. Much of it just fades into the wind. The great music endures with its power to enlarge our horizons beyond the present.

The Shawshank Redemption, a film based on a story by Stephen King, featured Tim Robbins as Andy Duffresne, a man wrongly convicted of murdering his wife. Morgan Freeman played the role of Red Redding, a prisoner who as a youth forty years before had been convicted of murder. In prison the two became friends. Andy manages after years of letter writing to secure state funds to furnish a prison library. One day he plays a record over the prison public address system, a soprano duet from the *Marriage of Figaro* by Mozart. The whole prison population grew silent and listened, those at work in the shops, those in the yard, those in the infirmary. The warden was angered and Andy ended up in solitary. Speaking of the influence of the music, Red said, "It was like some beautiful bird had come into our little cage and made those walls dissolve away, and for the moment every man at Shawshank felt free."

When Andy returned from solitary confinement his prison mates asked how it had gone. He told them, "I had Mozart to keep me company." "Did you tote that record player down there?" one of his buddies asked. Pointing to his head and heart Andy replied, "It's in here and here. That's the benefit of music. They can't take that away from you. It makes you remember places in the world that are not made of stone. There is something inside that they cannot touch. It's yours." When a friend asked what he was talking about, Andy said simply, "Hope!"

One sort of music that abides for many is jazz. I recently had occasion to ask a friend what he intended to do on vacation. "Listen to my jazz albums," he replied. Those of you who find similar nourishment in jazz may remember the film story of Dale Turner, a solo saxophonist. The film was *Round Midnight*. One scene is set in a jazz club. The time is a late October evening around midnight. The musicians are on break and the patrons are doing whatever patrons do during a break in the music. Dale goes out in the alley behind the club just to be by himself. When the musicians return to resume playing, Dale does not return. One of them goes out to look for him to see if he is all right. Dale answers him, "I am so weary; I'm tired of everything except the music."

Some music lasts and Heller's David had the right of it. David's psalms have lasted. There are two different estimates of David in the biblical narratives. In the narratives of Samuel we meet him as he was. He was many things: passionate, politically astute, devout, deceitful, loyal, self-serving, capable of magnanimous gestures, capable too of arranging a man's death, a public success, a private failure with public consequences, compassionate yet also vindictive. That's a mix of attributes, isn't it? Aren't we all a mix? The narrative in Samuel is unsparing when it comes to revealing the clay feet of David. The dark side of life is not glossed over.

There is another view of David that comes through loud and clear in the biblical books of Chronicles. The story of David, Bathsheba, and David's complicity in the death of her husband, Uriah, is omitted. Chronicles tells of another side of David. The Priestly writers tell of David's plans for the new temple, his organizing of the priesthood, and his institution of music in the liturgy. Chronicles recognizes David's capacity for deep devotion and credits him as the patron of sacred music. If David's horns are visible in Samuel, his halo shines forth in Chronicles. But then, again, aren't we all a mix of horns and haloes?

David composed and sang psalms: psalms of lament, thanksgiving, complaint; psalms that are prayers for deliverance, and others that are pleas for Divine mercy. Some are surely present in the Book of Psalms even though most were probably composed by others over the long and volatile history of the community of faith. Just surf through the Book of Psalms and note how the liturgists of Israel tied many to events in the life of David. In Israel the many-faceted David became the representative of all of us who face threats from enemies within and without, sin and suffer for our sins, hope against hope and despite our contradictions and frailty seek to continue living before God.

Do you recall the film, *Amadeus*, that won praises several years ago? It was the story of Wolfgang Amadeus Mozart. Mozart's music was much better than he was. That is true of us also. Our music and our hymns are much better than we are. But, reflect! Amadeus means "love of God." There is the interpretive key not only to Mozart's story and David's story, but also to ours. Grace reigns and that's what our hymns and anthems are all about. Here are lyrics that span the centuries, lyrics for life, lyrics for the times of sunrise and times when it's 'round midnight.

I leave with you these lines from an ancient hymn of the church, "Jerusalem, My Happy Home."

There David stands with harp in hand
As master of the choir;
Ten thousand times that one were blest
That might this music hear.

There Mary sings Magnificat
With tune surpassing sweet;
And all the sisters bear their part,
Sitting about her feet.

---

1. Heller, Joseph. *God Knows.* (Alfred A. Knopf: New York. 1984), p. 5.

2 Samuel 5:1-5, 9-10 Proper 9
Pentecost 7
Ordinary Time 14

Another Kind
Of Success

Rags-to-riches stories have been popular in every time and place. The story of Abraham Lincoln whose life led from the log cabin to the White House is a staple of Americana. So are the stories of Horatio Alger. He started writing just after the civil war. He wrote exclusively about underprivileged young people who through honesty, preseverance, and diligence went on to win fame and wealth. *Ragged Dick* and *Tattered Tom* were just two of the heroes he wrote about in over a hundred dime novels. Nearer to our own time are the rags-to-riches stories of two real life people. Lorreta Lynne, born a coal miner's daughter, became a star of country music. Elvis, the poor boy from Mississippi, became the king of rock and roll.

Just think about the enduring appeal of these rags-to-riches stories. Who among us has not fantasized about making it big? The people who run the big money sweepstakes know that we do. So do those who invest in gambling casinos and promote state lotteries. A television promo for the Megabucks lottery in Massachusetts showed a washerwoman in a large bank who, after winning big, walked into the boardroom of the bank, set aside her mop and bucket, and announced to the assembled officers of the bank, "Ladies and Gentlemen, I am sure you will enjoy working for me as much as I have enjoyed working for you." Here is the universal fantasy. Why do stories like *Treasure Island* and *Cinderella* retain an enduring appeal to children?

Here is the odd quirk. We cherish the memory of log cabin beginnings but we are not content with simplicity. It's the life styles of the rich and famous that evoke popular curiosity and adulation. A modern realtor wouldn't even classify a log cabin as a starter home. Upward mobility is the name of the game. But which way is up? And what about those in our land whose ongoing poverty traps them in a time warp in which there is neither past nor future, only the daily struggle to survive?

Even back in the iron age rags-to-riches stories were popular. Today's first reading is a shining example. David, the obscure shepherd boy, became the king of Israel. The child's hand that held a shepherd's crook became the adult hand that held the royal scepter. David became a popular folk hero invested with a larger-than-life image in later years after the nation went to pieces and became a land occupied by a succession of conquerors. How they dreamed that another David might rise and make them a nation once again. In the popular imagination David became enshrined as Israel's warrior celebrity par excellence.

"And David became greater and greater, for the Lord, the God of hosts, was with him." This comment which concludes today's reading tells us something about the way the teachers of Israel thought about people who attained position and means. The old orthodoxy of the book of Deuteronomy shines forth here. God rewards piety. Position and the trappings of success were equated with blessing. Human proficiency reflected God power. That's the way ancient folk thought about the attainment of celebrity status. If someone became famous, people looked for the Spirit of God at work in him. Today we look for his press agent and image consultant.

Jesus consigned the old orthodoxy of Deuteronomy to the wastebasket in his parable of the rich fool. Speaking of a rich fool was a contradiction in terms according to the old piety. Yet that old piety lingers on among us in our cultural definitions that define the good life as having the goods. Jesus took a traditional type of success story and put a different twist to it in one of his twin parables of the buried treasure and the pearl of great price. Listen to them.

> *The kingdom of heaven is like treasure hidden in a field which someone found and hid; then in his joy he goes and sells all that he has and buys that field.*
> *Again, the kingdom of heaven is like a merchant in search of fine pearls; on finding one pearl of great value, he went and sold all that he had and bought it.*
> — Matthew 13:44-45

The peasant shared the universal fantasy of making it big. The rich man who had made it bigger still sought more. Someone once asked John D. Rockefeller how much money it took to make someone happy. He replied, "Just a little more." Note the way the parables veer from the traditional plot of the success story. The listener would expect the peasant to make a big splash with a palatial house, designer clothes, a fancy stable, and a retinue of servants. The rich man would go on to amass more wealth and power. But that's not the way the versions of Jesus go. These are kingdom stories and the burden of these stories is another kind of wealth and another kind of success — making it big as a human being in whatever circle we walk, large or small.

2 Samuel 6:1-5, 12b-19   Proper 10
                                         Pentecost 8
                                      Ordinary Time 15

The Strange Tactics Of God

Some of you will remember *Indiana Jones And The Raiders Of The Lost Ark*, a film released several years ago but still showing up from time to time on cable and satellite television movie channels. Today we are going to trace a bit of the history of the ark as reported in 1 Samuel 4-6. We will not experience any of the dangers faced by Indiana Jones. We will encounter some marvelous Hebrew satire as well as some profound insight into the strange ways of God. But before starting I want to lift up two enigmatic texts and peg them in the air so that they hover over our thought.

Here is a verse from Psalm 78. The Psalmist is reflecting on the capture of the ark by the Philistines.

> *He abandoned his dwelling at Shiloh,*
> *the tent where he dwelt among mortals,*
> *and delivered his power to captivity,*
> *his glory to the hand of the foe.*
>   — Psalm 78:60

Here is another comment by a New Testament writer who is reflecting on the strange victory of God hidden in the defeat of Jesus on the cross.

> *When he ascended on high he made captivity itself a captive; he gave gifts to his people.*
>
> — Ephesians 4:8b

There they are. Just put them on a back burner and we will retrieve them later. Right now, rivet your attention on one of the unique and independent narratives of the Old Testament, the history of the Ark of God.

I do not know why they called it an ark. It was actually a rectangular wooden box measuring about six feet by three. There were carved winged creatures on the side representing the hosts of heaven. The ark rested on long poles so it could be carried. As the Israelites made their way through the wilderness, the ark was carried at the head of the column. At night it rested in the camp. When they entered Canaan, the ark led the way.

This imagery was much on the mind of the American poet John Greenleaf Whittier, who celebrated in poetry the trek of the antislavery emigrants from New England who settled in Kansas in the 1850s.

> *Upbearing like the Ark of old,*
> *The Bible in our van,*
> *We go to test the truth of God*
> *Against the fraud of man.*
>   — John Greenleaf Whittier, "The Kansas Emigrants"

When the Israelites entered Canaan and became a settled people, they set up shrines. The ark was deposited and tenderly cared for in the Shrine at Shiloh. What was in the ark? We do not know. The ark was the throne of Israel's invisible God. Wherever the ark was, there God was fully present. When the ark was raised and carried, there God marched with his people. That is what they believed. The ark was the grand symbol of God's presence with his people. It was an event charged with emotion when David danced before the ark as he brought it into Jerusalem.

But we are ahead of the story. Stay with this idea of the ark as a sign of a Divine guarantee and favor that can be held in human hands. The Israelites experienced a major shock when they carried the ark into battle against the Philistines, the well-armed folk who held the coastal plain and were determined the Israelites would not occupy their land.

It came about this way. Reeling from a thumping defeat, the Israelites retrieved the ark from Shiloh and brought it into their camp to the accompaniment of cheers and shouts. If you wonder at the effect of a wooden box on their morale, think of our own dependence on physical objects. I do not know about your peculiarities, but I do know about my own. If I arrive in the church office and discover I have left my briefcase or favorite pen at home, I feel handicapped for the day. I may never open the briefcase but its physical presence is somehow important to me. Linus goes around with his security blanket. Can you think of some tool or object that has morale value to you? In a larger dimension, we could list an automobile, possessions, a house. A community can feed its morale through certain buildings or monuments that gather a symbolic value about them: the White House, the Capitol dome, a church steeple. There are some things that have supportive meaning for us.

The arrival of the ark had an immediate effect upon the Israelite soldiers. The sight of the ark in the camp also struck fear in the hearts of the Philistines. "When they learned the ark of the Lord had come to the camp, the Philistines were afraid; for they said, 'Their God has come into the camp to them. Woe to us ... Nothing like this has happened before ... Who can deliver us from the power of this mighty God? ... Acquit yourselves like men, O Philistines ... and fight' " (1 Samuel 4:5-9).

The Philistines fought well, so well that the Israelites were routed and the ark captured. It was a disaster of major dimensions and news of the capture of the ark literally knocked Eli, the aged priest, dead. His daughter-in-law spoke for all when she lamented, "The glory has departed from Israel, for the ark of God has been captured." Her lament calls to mind the tear-filled words of Mary Magdalene. "They have taken away my Lord."

But this is not the end of the story of the ark. In the writer's perspective, this was a defeat of God's people, not of God. The focus of the story shifts to the fate of the ark in the land of the heathen. Flushed by their victory over the God of the Israelites, they set the ark up as a trophy in the house of their god, Dagon. But the next day Dagon is found face down in a position of homage before the ark. They set Dagon upright. The next day not only is Dagon found face down, but also his head and hands have been chopped off. Not only that, but the people of Ashdod begin to be afflicted with boils in embarrassing places. Then hordes of mice show up in the fields and start nibbling everything in sight.

The ark is moved to Gath. The same things start happening there. They send it to Ekron and the same results ensue. What to do with the ark is something like the problem of disposing of radioactive waste. Even when it got back into Israelite hands there were problems and not even some of the Israelites wanted it around.

This is the intriguing part of the story. There is a raw kind of humor and ridicule at work. God, as it were, with a flick of his finger is confusing everybody. But in the humor a profound insight is seeking expression, an insight forged out of the crucible of defeat and disaster. They had brought the ark into the camp and marched to war with it. But was God's blessing on their regiments and their cause? And for the Philistines, might did not make right either. Is there not a larger framework to history or such a reality as a God who refuses to be either bound, humanly programmed, or captured, or kept in some private box, or domesticated in some private chapel subservient to idols?

Is there not such a reality as a God who acts in history without favor, humbles human pretensions, and at times confounds his church? He is bigger than any box, any creed, any particularity. He refuses to be held hostage to any particular slant. It is interesting to note that the ark made its way back to Israel unexpectedly and surprisingly without any rescue mission being mounted. God seems to do quite well on his own. One day the people of Bethshemish look up as they are in the fields and there coming toward them is the ark in a cart laden with golden mice and golden tumors and drawn by milk cows.

Remember that the writers of this story of the ark were writing for posterity, for a people who would lose their shrines to Assyrian invasion, see their temple burned once by the Babylonians and again by the Romans, a people whose land would be occupied by others. But it was also written for us who have been made sons and daughters of Abraham and made privy to the Word. Here is the thrust in the story that speaks to us of the God beyond the occasions of defeat and confusion. All of our treasured symbols will ultimately be torn from our hands, but God is not in the symbols. The old war God of Israel died on the field of battle in this story. He had to die; his time had come. He had to go so that the God behind God might make himself known to his people: the true God, bigger than any box. He takes the field of history by delivering himself up. He has his own strange tactics. Listen! We are back at the beginning of this sermon. It's time to retrieve the two texts left hovering in the air.

Recall the words of the Psalmist as he broods over the strange tactics of God in history.

> *He abandoned his dwelling at Shiloh,*
> *the tent where he dwelt among mortals,*
> *and delivered his power to captivity,*
> *his glory to the hand of the foe.*

This is the Psalmist's poetic interpretation of the story we have been retelling, the capture and return of the ark. A strange and hard thought is surfacing here. God foregoes all his power in order to show that he is indeed God. This is the puzzling and incomprehensible mystery that found its embodiment in the story of Jesus. The end of the human way is not the end of God's way.

Recall the words of the writer of the letter to the Ephesians.

> *When he ascended on high he made captivity itself a captive; he gave gifts to his people.*

The God who let the ark go into captivity let's his Son be taken by the principalities and powers. The cross in human hands is a way of writing *finished* to the story of Jesus. But before long, rumors of a defeated God still alive begin to circulate. From here and there in the empire reports are heard. "Those who have turned the world upside down have come here also." Shades of the Philistines and the ark. There are mice in the grain fields, vexatious boils in the social body. What they thought they had stopped, defeated and routed from the field of history cannot be stopped. Captivity has been taken captive.

David brought the ark into Jerusalem. Solomon built a temple around it. It was destroyed when the Chaldeans razed the temple. It disappears from history. There is just one last mention of it in the Bible. John, in prison on the island of Patmos, catches a vision of eternity. "Then God's temple in heaven was opened, and the ark of his covenant was seen within his temple; and there were flashes of lightning, rumblings, peals of thunder, and earthquake, and heavy hail" (Revelation 11:19). In the end — God! His promise! His victory!

2 Samuel 7:1-14a   Proper 11
                                  Pentecost 9
                              Ordinary Time 16

A Habitat For Humanity

The God who made the world and everything in it, he who is Lord of heaven and earth, does not live in shrines made by human hands, nor is he served by human hands, as though he needed anything, since he himself gives to all mortals life and breath and all things. From one ancestor he made all nations to inhabit the whole earth.
— Acts 17:24-26b

Shortly after the death of F. Scott Fitzgerald some of his close friends went through his papers and manuscripts. They discovered a number of proposed plots for stories. One such plot dealt with the varied members of a family who had inherited a house. The bequest had one stipulation. To receive possession of the house they had to live in it harmoniously and purposefully.

That's quite a stipulation. Living together in harmony is no easy task in any house large or small. The testator in Fitzgerald's proposed plot doesn't leave any margin for error. It's simply get along or get out! Fortunately for us and our larger human family on this earth, God has not given us an eviction notice, at least, not yet. That in part is what grace is all about. It also says something about what the scriptures call the patience and forbearance of God.

In these mid years of the premillennial decade I sense in a good many folks I talk with something of a doomsday mood. No one seems to be bullish about the future. Brood long enough about the massive human problems of the planet and it is difficult not to become depressed. The conflicts and tensions just go on and on. Old rivalries and divisions continue to plague the social fabric of the world. If the great question of the sixteenth century was "Where can I find a gracious God?" the burning question at the end of this turbulent twentieth century is "Where can I find a gracious neighbor?"

The desire for supportive community exists in all of us. Several years ago an interesting experiment involving children was conducted at the University of Louvain in Belgium. A group was shown three pictures of a birthday celebration. The first showed a child all alone with cake, ice cream, and a pile of toys. The second showed a child with mother and father, cake, ice cream, and toys. The third showed a child with mother, father, and a lot of other people around a table with lots of food. There were no toys.

The children were asked to think of their own birthday and in terms of these pictures express their preference. None of the children selected the first scene. One out of three selected the second scene. Seventy-two percent of the boys and sixty-nine percent of the girls selected the third scene. These children were expressing a universal preference. We want a caring community around us.

But here is the paradox. While we want community we tend to be more comfortable with people just like our selves. There dwells also within us a fear of diversity. This is a contradiction we can observe in our own national history. The Statue of Liberty was given to us by the people of France to celebrate the one hundredth anniversary of our independence. We are all familiar with the words of the American writer, Emma Lazarus, appearing on a tablet in the main entrance to the pedestal. "Give me your tired, your poor, Your huddled masses yearning to breathe free, The wretched refuse of your teeming shores. Send these, the homeless, tempest-tossed to me, I lift my lamp beside the golden door!"

When the immigrants surged in during the latter part of the last century and the early part of this one, a pattern of people flight appeared. We didn't quite know how to relate to these folk with different languages and customs. It was difficult to understand a person's ambition to own a push cart or be a tailor. The urban flight began with the coming of the country day school, the country club, the upscale resort areas, and the exodus to the suburbs. This pattern has continued and still today we sense this fear of diversity.

One recent manifestation of this people fear is the advent of walled and gated suburban enclaves and the controlled environment of planned retirement communities. Celebration is the town to be built close to the Magic Kingdom in Disneyworld. A feature article in *USA Today* had this to say about it. "Celebration is billed as a 19th-century town for the late 20th century, harking back to a time when lemonade stands, not crime, were on every corner. Disney is selling turn-of-the century safety, charm and orderliness."[1]

This ambivalence about the contours of community crops up in our biblical narratives. Today's first reading is an example. God nixes David's plan to build a house for him. In turn God promises that he will build a house for David. It will not be a house of cedar wood or stone, but a community. In the biblical sense, a house can also mean a community that shares the purpose of its progenitor. God's house is the community that shares God's purpose. The promise is made that an offspring of David will come and build a house for God. But we note that the envisioned community is one bound by a common ethnic boundary.

The early Christians as they sought to understand the meaning of Jesus turned to passages like this to see him as the fulfiller of the promise. But in terms of what Jesus did and said the bounds of community were radically expanded beyond the litmus tests set down by race and piety. Geography was set aside as the gospel writers Christified space. Instead of a promised land every land became a land of promise. The vision at the heart of the New Testament is the vision of a diverse and inclusive community.

This particular narrative is part of what is called the succession narrative in the books of Samuel. It was written in a time when many felt things were just falling apart in Israel. But this is not a story that wallows in nostalgia. It tells of the days of David the way they were. The dark side of life is much in evidence as one reads on about the undercurrent of rivalry and corruption during the days of David. The whole document was a call to hold fast in all times to the promise and the vision. The last verse of chapter six should really be part of the reading, for that verse is the essential preface. "And Michal the daughter of Saul had no child to the day of her death." Remember, Michal was David's wife. Remember also that barrenness is biblical metaphor for the absence of visible assurances about the future. Prophetic promises are always made in the midst of contradiction and absurdity.

Driving along the coast of Spain not too long ago, we stopped at a walled overview to look out at the sea. I noted on the wall someone had drawn three symbols: the oval enclosed Serbian cross, the letters KKK, and a swastika. I would like to think it was just a bit of juvenile graffiti. But all three in their own way are symbols of the way human arrogance and people fear can presume to make God into a household patron. Neither the imprisoned cross, nor the fiery cross, nor the twisted cross represent the cross of him who died for all that all of us might be brothers and sisters in the household of God.

---

1. *USA Today*. October 18, 1995.

Lectionary Preaching After Pentecost

The following index will aid the user of this book in matching the correct Sunday with the appropriate text during Pentecost. All texts in this book are from the series for Lesson One, Revised Common Lectionary. (Note that the ELCA division of Lutheranism is now following the Revised Common Lectionary.) The Lutheran and Roman Catholic designations indicate days comparable to Sundays on which Revised Common Lectionary Propers are used.

(Fixed dates do not pertain to Lutheran Lectionary)

Fixed Date Lectionaries *Revised Common (including ELCA)* *and Roman Catholic*	Lutheran Lectionary *Lutheran*
The Day of Pentecost	The Day of Pentecost
The Holy Trinity	The Holy Trinity
May 29-June 4 — Proper 4, Ordinary Time 9	Pentecost 2
June 5-11 — Proper 5, Ordinary Time 10	Pentecost 3
June 12-18 — Proper 6, Ordinary Time 11	Pentecost 4
June 19-25 — Proper 7, Ordinary Time 12	Pentecost 5
June 26-July 2 — Proper 8, Ordinary Time 13	Pentecost 6
July 3-9 — Proper 9, Ordinary Time 14	Pentecost 7
July 10-16 — Proper 10, Ordinary Time 15	Pentecost 8
July 17-23 — Proper 11, Ordinary Time 16	Pentecost 9
July 24-30 — Proper 12, Ordinary Time 17	Pentecost 10
July 31-Aug. 6 — Proper 13, Ordinary Time 18	Pentecost 11
Aug. 7-13 — Proper 14, Ordinary Time 19	Pentecost 12
Aug. 14-20 — Proper 15, Ordinary Time 20	Pentecost 13
Aug. 21-27 — Proper 16, Ordinary Time 21	Pentecost 14
Aug. 28-Sept. 3 — Proper 17, Ordinary Time 22	Pentecost 15
Sept. 4-10 — Proper 18, Ordinary Time 23	Pentecost 16
Sept. 11-17 — Proper 19, Ordinary Time 24	Pentecost 17

Sept. 18-24 — Proper 20, Ordinary Time 25	Pentecost 18
Sept. 25-Oct. 1 — Proper 21, Ordinary Time 26	Pentecost 19
Oct. 2-8 — Proper 22, Ordinary Time 27	Pentecost 20
Oct. 9-15 — Proper 23, Ordinary Time 28	Pentecost 21
Oct. 16-22 — Proper 24, Ordinary Time 29	Pentecost 22
Oct. 23-29 — Proper 25, Ordinary Time 30	Pentecost 23
Oct. 30-Nov. 5 — Proper 26, Ordinary Time 31	Pentecost 24
Nov. 6-12 — Proper 27, Ordinary Time 32	Pentecost 25
Nov. 13-19 — Proper 28, Ordinary Time 33	Pentecost 26
	Pentecost 27
Nov. 20-26 — Christ the King	Christ the King

Reformation Day (or last Sunday in October) is October 31 (Revised Common, Lutheran)

All Saints' Day (or first Sunday in November) is November 1 (Revised Common, Lutheran, Roman Catholic)

Books In This Cycle B Series

Gospel Set

God's Downward Mobility
Sermons For Advent, Christmas And Epiphany
John A. Stroman

Which Way To Jesus?
Sermons For Lent And Easter
Harry N. Huxhold

Water Won't Quench The Fire
Sermons For Pentecost (First Third)
William G. Carter

Fringe, Front And Center
Sermons For Pentecost (Middle Third)
George W. Hoyer

No Box Seats In The Kingdom
Sermons For Pentecost (Last Third)
William G. Carter

First Lesson Set

Light In The Land Of Shadows
Sermons For Advent, Christmas And Epiphany
Harold C. Warlick, Jr.

Times Of Refreshing
Sermons For Lent and Easter
E. Carver McGriff

Lyrics For The Centuries
Sermons For Pentecost (First Third)
Arthur H. Kolsti

No Particular Place To Go
Sermons For Pentecost (Middle Third)
Timothy J. Smith

When Trouble Comes!
Sermons For Pentecost (Last Third)
Zan W. Holmes, Jr.